THE RAILWAYS OF
PEEBLES

ROY G. PERKINS

WITH IAIN MacINTOSH

Preface

The reader is asked to note, as in our previous book, that where possible equivalent contemporary views to the historic photographs have been provided. This has not always been feasible due to tree growth, new buildings or land reuse and new construction in some cases. Such cases are noted in the script where applicable. We apologies for such examples but a visit to the sites involved will illustrate the difficulties. The opportunity has also been taken to include more of the landscape north of Hardengreen Junction and entering into Galashiels south of Kilnknowe Junction. This is to aid a full description of a passenger journey over the route and illustrates well the engineering constraints faced by the original construction, particularly at Galashiels. Space constraints prevented a more detailed look at these in our previous book, *The Waverley Route Through Time*.

Roy G. Perkins

Iain MacIntosh

Front Cover

Top: The 'Farewell to Peebles' Railtour calls at Peebles Station behind J37 64587 on the day of the last passenger train, 3 February 1962. Two days later, on 5 February, the route from Kilnknowe Junction, Galashiels, to Rosewell & Hawthornden was to close officially. Rosewell and Hawthornden remained open to passenger traffic for a further seven months before itself succumbing. The line did remain open to Penicuik for freight until March 1967.

Bottom: The derelict buildings survived beyond the line's closure and were still extent in disrepair into the late 1960s and early 1970s before being swept away for road improvements and the realigning of the A703. The goods yard and station forecourt became a car park conveniently located for Peebles town centre. Only the goods office and weigh bridge building survive at this time.

Back Cover

Top: The view from Plumbtreehall north to Kinlknowe Junction sees a short freight entering the town. This pre-1933 shot shows Kilnknowe Junction signal box above the bridge over Gala Water. Wheatlands Mill stands in the background.

Bottom: The same view in 2013 with vegetation clearance complete and the soon to be removed 'Black path' along the former route. Trains should return to service here again in 2015.

First published 2013

Amberley Publishing
The Hill, Stroud, Gloucestershire, GL5 4EP
www.amberley-books.com

Copyright © Roy Perkins and Iain MacIntosh, 2013

The right of Roy Perkins and Iain MacIntosh to be identified as the Authors of this work has been asserted in accordance with the Copyrights, Designs and Patents Act 1988.

ISBN 978 1 4456 1387 1 (print)
ISBN 978 1 4456 1395 6 (ebook)

British Library Cataloguing in Publication Data.
A catalogue record for this book is available from the British Library.

Typesetting by Amberley Publishing.
Printed in Great Britain.

Introduction

North British opened the Edinburgh & Hawick Railway, precursor of the Waverley Route. In opening the Hawick line, the North British laid a claim to railway hegemony in the Borders which it never relinquished despite protracted and concerted efforts by the Caledonian Railway both around Peebles and to the south of Hawick. Even before the opening by the North British of the Berwick via Drem route to Edinburgh, the Caledonian Railway had proposed a line from Ayr to Berwick via Douglas, Peebles and Kelso, but like many other Railway Mania schemes it had come to naught. If the original need or demand for the Waverley Route from the Central Borders to Edinburgh was fuelled by Edinburgh's seemingly insatiable appetite for coal then the requirement for the railways from Peebles was quite the opposite. Peebles' interest in a railway was far more parochial.

Peebles had featured in railway proposals from very early in the nineteenth century, some of them now quite strange to us. Take, for example, the proposed line from Berwick to Glasgow proposed by none other than Thomas Telford (a native of Westerkirk, near Langholm) in 1810 and the similar scheme put forward by no less than Robert Stephenson in 1821. These schemes came to nothing, as did a number of other plans proposed during the 1830s and 1840s for railways linking Newcastle with Edinburgh and Glasgow via Peebles. Such was the intensity of the rivalry to provide a railway route over the Anglo-Scottish border that a Royal Commission was set up to report on the rival schemes. This commission reported in 1841 and decided that only one route was needed and that that route should be the one proposed by the Caledonian Railway Company from Glasgow to Carlisle via Beattock, with a branch from Carstairs serving Edinburgh by way of nowhere in particular. In spite of these findings the North British Railway pressed on with its preferred route via Drem and Berwick, which it opened in 1846. Two years later, the Caledonian Railway opened their route from Glasgow to Carlisle via Beattock. In 1847 the Caledonian obtained Parliamentary powers to build a line from Symington to Broughton but these powers were allowed to lapse. In 1849, the same fate awaited a locally promoted 1845 scheme for a line from Peebles to Edinburgh by way of Penicuik.

This situation remained the same until 1851 and Peebles was in danger of languishing as a communication backwater while its near neighbours, Galashiels and Hawick, prospered with their railway lines. In 1851 three local 'worthies', William Chambers, Walter Thorburn and John Bathgate, seeing the town's competitive situation worsening, decided to take action themselves and proposed a local company which was to build a line as cheaply as possible. To this end, the services of Thomas Bouch were retained to survey a route from Eskbank, on the Edinburgh & Hawick Railway, through Bonnyrigg, Hawthornden and Leadburn and thence down Eddlestone Water to Peebles – a distance of about 18.75 miles. A capital for the original company of some £70,000 was proscribed, with powers to raise additional loans of £23,000. Bouch, who would later become Sir Thomas Bouch and achieve note for his part in construction of the Tay Bridge, was as good as his word and the line duly opened on 4 July 1855. The Peebles Railway, as it became, was to remain independent, despite various courtships, until it became vested in the North British Railway by an Act of Parliament of 13 July 1876.

However, to return to the opening of the Peebles Railway, the fledgling railway did not have an easy birth. Initially the Board of Trade wrote to say that the line and works would be inspected on its behalf by Captain Tyler RE on 28 June 1855 and the Board of Directors dutifully arranged for their latest locomotive, *Tweed*, to pull first class carriages to Eskbank to meet him. They also arranged for lunch to be provided at the Tontine Hotel from 12.00 to 1.00 p.m. The inspector was duly collected from Eskbank and proceeded to inspect the works. The inspection was completed and Captain Tyler announced himself very satisfied with the railway. That, however, was not the end of the story because on 2 July 1855 a letter was received from the Board of Trade announcing that they would only agree to the opening of the railway provided that a system of 'one engine in steam' was implemented. This was clearly impractical given that the line was nearly nineteen miles long. The company was already starting to pay the price for Thomas Bouch's inexpensive railway. No passing loops had been provided on the line, meaning that if trains were to pass each other, one or other had to be shunted off the running line into a siding. The Peebles Railway's directors were anxious to start operating their trains, however, and negotiations were rapidly instituted with the board of Trade, culminating in an agreement with the Board that the railway could be operated with the use of pilotmen, the route being divided into two at Pomathorn so that one pilotman operated between Eskbank and Pomathorn and the other between Pomathorn and Peebles. It was announced that public services would start on Wednesday 4 July 1855. This was the result of the Peebles Railway's initiative and was acted on before agreement from the Board of Trade had been received. That agreement was duly received in late July, by which time the railway had been operational for nearly a month.

The opening of the railway took place as announced but it was probably one of the lowest profile openings of any railway in Britain. There was no ceremony or fanfare as the first train steamed out of the company's March Street terminus, quite unlike the ceremony attaching to the 'cutting of the first sod' on 9 August 1853, some two years earlier. However, despite the lack of ceremony the first train was extremely well patronised. In the first week the passenger revenue was nearly £53 and by the week ending 18 August 1855 it was almost £167.

Three passenger trains a day were operated between Peebles and Edinburgh and the same number on the return. Coaches belonging to the PR were attached to the rear of NBR trains at the Edinburgh station and were detached at Eskbank, where a PR locomotive took over for the rest of the journey. There matters rested while the Peebles Railway enjoyed six years of independence despite periodic attempts by the North British Railway to take it over.

On 1 February 1861, the Peebles Railway accepted the North British Railway's offer to take over the running and maintenance of the line, selling all its rolling stock and locomotives to the NBR for £20,000. The spectre of competition, however, raised its head on 23 May 1858 with the incorporation of the Symington, Biggar & Broughton Railway for a line from a junction with Caledonian Railway's main line from Glasgow to Carlisle at Symington through Biggar to Broughton. This probably seemed innocuous enough to the directors of the Peebles Railway; in any event they, do not appear to have reacted. It's fair to say that the purpose of this line and the source of its funding were hidden from the Peebles directors – it was only later that it became clear that the Caledonian were behind the scheme. On 5 November 1860 the Symington, Biggar & Broughton opened its line to a terminus at Broughton. Meanwhile, on 3 July 1860 the Symington company was granted parliamentary permission to extend its line from Broughton into Peebles while on 1 July 1861 the Symington, Biggar & Broughton Railway was formally absorbed by the Caledonian Railway.

If the directors of the Peebles railway seem to have ignored the imminent threat from the Symington, Biggar & Broughton Railway, the North British Railway's directors were evidently watching the situation closely because on 28 June 1861, just three days before the Symington Company was formally amalgamated with the Caledonian Railway, the North British Railway was empowered to build a line from Galashiels to Peebles, through Clovenfords, Walkerburn and Innerleithen, thus blocking any attempt by the Caledonian Railway to penetrate further into what, as we have seen, the North British regarded as its fiefdom. Thus ended the railway battle for Peebles, not with a bang but a whimper.

Description of the Routes

From the point of view of a passenger, the most southerly station on the Waverley Route to be served by trains of the Peebles Railway was Eskbank, while from an operational viewpoint it was Hardengreen Junction. This was because while Hardengreen was further south, it provided no facilities for passengers – Eskbank was the most southerly point at which that could be accomplished. The first station on the Peebles Railway itself was Bonnyrigg, which actually opened in August 1855, a month after the rest of the railway and something of an afterthought. The North British Railway had thought that Bonnyrigg warranted a station at the planning stage of the Peebles Railway but the Peebles directors had not agreed. In June 1855 the Peebles directors, no doubt influenced by the prospects for passenger traffic, agreed and instructed Thomas Bouch to build one. The station was originally built with one platform but later gained a second, placed opposite the other, including station buildings and a crossing keeper's cottage adjacent to the Bonnyrigg level crossing. There was also a footbridge and signal cabin and at this stage a single siding comprised the goods yard, which was later expanded. In the early days of the PR the line was single throughout but on 15 April 1867 the Esk Valley Railway, a new branch to Polton, led to the line being doubled from Hardengreen to Esk Valley Junction, a little short of Bonnyrigg. The first station on the new line was also named Bonnyrigg, causing the Peebles station to be renamed Bonnyrigg Road until the Esk Valley station was renamed Broomieknowe in 1868 and the PR station reverted to its original name.

Progressing further uphill, the little line ploughed its furrow to Rosewell & Hawthornden station, which was opened at the same time as the Peebles Railway's main line, on 4 July

1855. Over the years, there was considerable discussion and dispute regarding the name of the station. It was originally to be called Gortonlee, which is actually somewhat closer to the site than Hawthornden, but opened as Hawthornden. All dispute appears to have been accommodated on 9 July 1928, when it was renamed Rosewell & Hawthornden. The station itself latterly comprised two platforms standing directly opposite each other. On the down platform was an unprepossessing single-storey building containing a general and a ladies' waiting room and the booking office. There was also a slightly lower extension to this building at the eastern end containing a gents' toilet. On the opposing or up platform was a waiting room, timber-built on a stone base. There was also a signal box situated on the down side, at the entrance to the goods yard, and a footbridge linking the two platforms. By the 1950s two loops had been added either side of the down platform, necessitating another footbridge to provide direct access to Rosewell village. At both ends of the down platform were loading docks used by freight trains. The line was later doubled from Esk Valley Junction to Rosewell.

About a quarter of a mile west of Rosewell & Hawthornden station was Gorton level crossing and a little beyond that stood Hawthornden Junction, where from 1872 the Penicuik Branch diverged to the right and sidings associated with Whitehill collieries to the left.

Still climbing, the next station on the line was Rosslynlee. Like Rosewell & Hawthornden, this had opened with the rest of the Peebles Railway on 4 July 1855 and like Rosewell & Hawthornden, the name of the station was subject to dispute. It was originally to have been named Kirkettle but on opening was actually styled Roslin. In 1864 it was renamed Rosslyn and in 1872, after pressure from the NBR, finally renamed Rosslynlee.

A short distance beyond Rosslynlee Station was the short-lived Rosslynlee Hospital Halt. This halt was opened in December 1958 to serve, as its name suggests, Rosslynlee Hospital, though the hospital had had its own siding for many years. Known as Holm Bank siding (there were various spellings), it was used mainly to deliver coal for the hospital boilers and its own gasworks. Built to a strict budget and of timber and cinder construction, the halt accommodated an open-fronted waiting shed and tickets were sold at the hospital itself by the Hospital Steward. It was the responsibility, for railway purposes, of the stationmaster at Rosewell & Hawthornden, who collected the ticket revenue twice a week. Still heading west, the line crossed the Auchendinny–Howgate road (now the B7026) on the level at Loanstone, where the crossing keeper's cottage and small signal cabin can still be seen. Just before the line crossed the road there were two sidings, used for agricultural purposes.

Sited on the down side of the line, to the north of the level crossing, Pomathorn only ever had the one platform, sited on the north side of the B6372. In addition, at the south end of the station there was a substantial single-storey stationmaster's house, built of stone with a pitched roof, which stood at right angles to the platform. The station building itself was also built of stone with a slate roof. It housed a general and a ladies' waiting room as well as toilets and a ticket office. There was a small signal box at the southern end of the station, which served to control the adjacent level crossing, as a well as a somewhat larger example toward the northern end, controlling the access to the three-siding goods yard. This goods yard boasted a loading dock complete with end-loading facility as well as a two ton yard crane. Until the opening in 1872 of the

Penicuik Branch this station was titled Penicuik but from then was accorded the title Pomathorn for Penicuik, which it bore for the rest of its existence. The station became an unstaffed halt from 1 November 1946.

Still travelling uphill, the line next came to its summit at Leadburn. Leadburn Station, later Leadburn Junction, was opened with the rest of the line on 4 July 1855 and served no substantial population centre; in fact, it was little more than a crossroads and an inn, though it also boasted a very early example of road/rail integration, with coaches taking passengers forward to West Linton, Romanno Bridge and Broughton. Leadburn continued this lonely existence until 4 July 1864, when the Leadburn, Linton & Dolphinton Railway opened to traffic. Officially the station was always known as Leadburn, even though some Ordnance Survey maps described it as Leadburn Junction. With the coming of the LL&DR, a new bay platform was created on the west side of the down platform. The line to Peebles had two platforms not quite opposite each other; the principal station buildings were on the down platform and contained waiting rooms and toilets while the up platform had a small waiting room and was fitted with a hipped slate roof and a narrow canopy. Close to these two buildings, a wooden footbridge linked the two platforms. The aforementioned bay platform had a passing loop with, at its northern end, a turntable which was used by the LL&DR locomotives, which were stabled at Dolphinton. There was a long refuge siding behind the up platform (later a loop) and the goods yard, with two sidings which both served a loading dock, was located at the north-western end of the station, where the stationmaster's house also was. Beyond the southern extremity of the down platform was situated the original signal box, which was replaced in 1892 by a new box close by the footbridge on the down platform. This signal box was demolished in 1953, being replaced by a simple single-storey, brick-built structure. There were also watering facilities here, with a water tank at the east side of the up siding and a water column at the north end of the down platform. The station was closed to passengers from 7 March 1955, though it remained in use as a crossing place.

After crossing the Peebles road and just after the point at which the LL&DR headed west across the moors, at the summit of the line, there was originally a siding, facing towards Peebles. This was used in the early days of the line, when the locomotives were not powerful enough to haul many loaded coal trucks. Half a train of coal would be left in the siding and the locomotive would later return with the rest, taking the whole train down to Peebles. Returning, the wagons would be empty and the locomotive could pull the whole train back. It had gone by 1897 though the OS map still shows the widening of the company fence, showing where it was situated.

As the railway starts its gradient downhill toward Peebles, the next stop was at Earlyvale Gate. The Peebles Railway directors had no intention at the time of construction of providing a stop at Earlyvale Gate, let alone a station. However, they reckoned without James Hay McKenzie, who in July 1856 wrote to the Peebles Railway directors. McKenzie asked the directors to provide a station at Earlyvale Gate for the benefit of his friend Mr George Dundas, who was soon to move to Cowie's Llyn near Earlyvale Gate. In return for this concession, Dundas promised traffic from his suppliers as well as from his friends and family using the new railway. Perhaps unsurprisingly, the railway's directors declined to provide a station for just one family but did agree that trains would stop here at a signal, mornings and evenings on market days (Tuesdays, Wednesdays and Thursdays), provided that Mr Dundas bought a season ticket from Eddleston to Edinburgh. So it came about that Earlyvale Gate became a stop but not a station, rather akin to Nook Pasture on the Waverley Route proper. Even so, Earlyvale Gate had a brief lifespan, first appearing in public timetables in June 1856 and not appearing again after February 1857.

Continuing southward, the next station was at Eddleston, some four miles from Peebles and twenty miles from Edinburgh. Eddleston was a planned village of some 800 souls, laid out grid-style by Lord Elibank in the eighteenth century. Initially the station had only one platform, situated on the up side of the line. Atop this platform stood the station building, a rectangular structure built of brick and surmounted by a pitched slate roof. Inside, the building contained a booking office as well as ladies' and general waiting rooms; at the south end of the building was a gentlemen's toilet. At some time in the 1890s, the station was further developed by the building of another platform on the down side opposite the existing northbound platform, together with a wooden footbridge linking the two. A further development came with the provision in 1895 of a new signal box controlling both the level crossing at the north end of the station and the access to the small two-siding goods yard. This goods yard had loading banks and a two-ton crane. There was also a stone-built stationmaster's house close to the level crossing. The last leg of the railway as originally built took the permanent way into Peebles itself.

Peebles Station as originally constructed was located on a rather cramped site in March Street, Peebles. It was located to the west of a mill-race which flowed southward from Eddleston Water. The passenger station was stone-built and stood adjacent to a timber-built goods shed. Passengers climbed a short flight of stairs to gain access to the building and once inside could turn either to the right, for the booking office and lamp room, or to the left for the toilets and a gents' urinal. The station had only one platform and along part of its length stood a trainshed or overall roof, but it also provided an engine release loop. The far side of the trainshed shared a supporting wall with the goods shed. There were only two sidings in the goods yard, one stopping short of the goods shed and the other passing straight though it, across March Street and onward to a saw-mill. When the station was built, the opportunity was taken to build on the approach a single-road locomotive shed, which in the early days of the PR also served as a workshop where locomotives and stock were maintained.

The second approach by railway toward Peebles came from the west, in the form of the Symington, Biggar & Broughton Railway. This line, initially of some eight miles, began at a junction with the Caledonian Railway at Symington in Lanarkshire and ran via stations at Coulter and Biggar to Broughton in the Scottish Borders. Initially the line ran only to Broughton, where the company established its headquarters, but before long the company showed its true colours when an application was made to Parliament for an extension of the line to Peebles. (The fact that the Caledonian Railway had subscribed £7,500 toward the company's original capital of £36,000 had apparently escaped the notice of the directors of the Peebles Railway). However, be that as it may, the extension of the SB&BR to Peebles was duly sanctioned on 3 July 1860. The 11¼-mile extension of the original line was duly constructed and opened on 1 February 1864 to a new station in Peebles which was later to be styled Peebles West. The North British Railway had been assiduously courting the Peebles Railway for some years and was considerably chagrined by these developments. However, the North British may have been disappointed but they were by no means defeated and immediately set about retaliation. Application was made to Parliament and by an Act dated 28 June 1861 the North British Railway was duly empowered to build an eighteen-mile line from Galashiels on its Hawick branch to Peebles by way of Cardrona, Innerleithen, Walkerburn and Clovenfords to Peebles. In securing and building this line, the North British had effectively maintained its hegemony of the Scottish Borders because even the most imaginative promoters could not find a case for two railways between Peebles and Galashiels. For the time being, the fierce rivalry between the Caledonian Railway and the North British was at an end. To return, however, to the Symington, Biggar & Broughton Railway, from its junction with the Caledonian Railway at Symington the line forged broadly eastward via Coulter to Biggar, South Lanarkshire and the Coulter Viaduct over the River Clyde. Biggar, population in 2011 2,301, was a relatively substantial station, as befitted the size of the village. The next stop was Broughton, population in 2011 some 306 and in those days the headquarters of the railway, where a station was opened on 5 November 1860. However, in 1897 Edinburgh & District Water Trust decided to construct a major reservoir in the area and, according to the needs of the day, they required rail access to the site. As the nearest railway, the SB&B, was some eight miles distant, it required a new railway to service the site as well as the doubling of the existing line to Broughton. The Edinburgh & District Water Trust embarked on the work itself as well as with the help of the Caledonian Railway and saw it through to a successful conclusion. The new railway started at Rachan Junction, just outside Broughton, and travelled some eight miles south, broadly parallel with the River Tweed and the A701 (road) to the construction headquarters at Victoria Lodge. The construction of the Talla Railway, as the line was known, was a pretty substantial affair, many traces of which still survive despite it having been destined for a short life, in railway terms. There were no intermediate stations between Rachan and Victoria Lodge until the opening of Crook Halt, some two miles north of Victoria Lodge. Crook Halt was the brainchild of James Best, a major sub-contractor in the Talla Railway's construction who had thoughtfully secured a financial stake in the nearby Crook Inn, one of Scotland's oldest licensed properties, if not in fact the oldest. In the event, the Talla Railway continued to operate until 1910. Progress continued to be made beyond Broughton and the single line to Peebles ploughed on via the villages of Stobo and Lyne, at both of which stations were constructed. On 1 August 1861 the Symington, Biggar & Broughton Railway, together with its westward extension into Peebles, was amalgamated with the Caledonian Railway. Thus the Caledonian Railway gained its only toehold within the Scottish Borders; it was, as already stated, to progress no further and indeed the Caledonian lines are outwith the scope of this current study.

However, that is by no means the end of the tale because, as has already been alluded to, the North British Railway had in 1861 secured the powers to construct another line to Peebles, this time from Galashiels.

Description of the Peebles–Galashiels Line
The extension to Galashiels was opened in two parts – the line as far as Innerleithen on 1 October 1864, and throughout to Galashiels on 18 June 1866. The new line by-passed the original Peebles station (which became goods only) and crossed over the Eddleston Water before passing under the main Edinburgh road to enter a narrow site at the foot of Venlaw Hill. Beyond the

single platform, the land opened out and was used to construct a new goods yard, much more conveniently situated for the town. The original 1864 station seems to have been somewhat camera-shy and was replaced by a fine modern red-brick building in 1905 which would go on to be featured on many postcards. The authorising Act had also made provision to build a connecting line to join up with the Caledonian Railway station on the other side of the Tweed, which had of course opened by 1864. It was to feature a triangular junction to enable trains to run from the Caledonian station to Galashiels (though the line as far as the Caledonian station was owned by the NBR). This new line was not ready by the time the Board of Trade inspector who inspected the line prior to its opening as far as Innerleithen made his report, but when he returned two years later it was; he noted that though the rails had been laid for the south-east chord, the points had been disconnected and recommended that they be restored. They probably never were, the NBR considering the cost of the construction of a short line they never intended to use a fair price to pay to deny any attempt by the Caledonian to establish running rights down the Tweed valley. The track was later lifted and the arch under the Innerleithen road blocked by a slatted wooden barrier which was still there until at least the late 1960s. The line to the Caledonian station was accessed by a sharp curve across the mouth of the new goods yard and controlled by a signal box called Peebles Junction, the signal box controlling the old station sidings being known as Peebles Engine Shed.

The line to the Caledonian station was used only for transferring stock between the two companies, though there is a record in 1936 of an excursion from Lanark to Melrose, made up of LMS stock and hauled throughout by an LMS locomotive, with the help of an LNER pilotman, using the line. Though unusual, this working was unlikely to have been unique. During the Second World War, storage facilities for Royal Navy shells were established on the moors served by the remains of the Leadburn, Linton & Dolphinton Railway, which had closed in 1933, and shells were often misdirected to 'the Dolphinton Branch', which no longer existed at that point, the track having being lifted from Dolphinton to Broomlee. The wagons ended up on the ex-Caledonian Dolphinton branch from Carstairs and had to be worked via the Peebles Caledonian station over the loop line towards Leadburn. The ex-Caledonian Peebles station was closed to passengers on 3 June 1950, and to goods on 7 June 1954, after which the line was lifted from the west end of Peebles station to Broughton. The station (which served Peebles cattle market and was also used to store redundant wagons and coaches) was retained and worked as a branch from Peebles Junction. The Caledonian station also had a much larger turntable (60 feet in diameter) than the one at the old Peebles station, which was only 36 feet in diameter, and engines often ran light to it to be turned.

Leaving Peebles and passing the signal box, the line passed under two bridges, both of which are still to be seen, (the second one having a wider arch, made to accommodate the now lifted chord of the triangular junction) before passing through the grounds of Peebles's famous Hydropathic Hotel, which provided much traffic for the line from its opening in 1880, passing over the road to Soonhope farm. This road led to a valley where many people had summer holiday cabins, many of which were former railway carriages. The line, then running parallel to the Innerleithen road, entered a cutting and then a short tunnel which took it under the road to pass Peebles Gasworks, which opened in 1905 and were served by a siding facing towards Innerleithen. The line then passed to the south of Horsburgh Keep before crossing the Tweed to enter Cardrona Station. With a population of barely 200, Cardrona did not warrant a substantial station and it did not get it. Indeed, the Board of Trade inspector commented that the facilities at the station should be improved, though nothing was done for nearly forty years after his comments were made. In 1895, however, the railway sprang into action and proposed a new station building and extended platform along with some re-alignment of the sidings in the goods yard. The new station building was of brick construction with a pitched slate roof and the standard North British wooden panelled face to the platform. However, it appears that the new building obstructed the view from the small, eight-lever signal box, the siting of which had to be marginally altered. The goods yard consisted of a single siding with a head-shunt which also served a loading dock.

As originally built, Innerleithen Station had only one platform, located on the up side of the line with a four-siding goods yard situated behind it. One of those sidings ran through the large brick-built, slate-roofed goods shed before passing a substantial loading dock. There were also cattle pens in the north-west corner of the goods yard as well as three short sidings on the down side of the running line. By the end of the nineteenth century the station had been considerably enlarged and now boasted a second, down platform, staggered by a half its length from the original up platform. By now two signal boxes were provided; one was on the down side, adjacent to the level crossing and opposite the up platform; and the other was a tall wooden structure on a brick base, located beyond the east end of the up platform and of a design that proved to be a signature of the Peebles loop, controlling access to the goods yard. The main station building was adjacent to the level crossing on the up side and consisted of a two-storey building built on an 'L' plan with a slate roof and a single-storey wing at its east end. Additionally, there was a large canopy which was supported on cast iron stanchions. The main station building comprised the stationmaster's accommodation, waiting rooms, booking office and toilets. On the down platform there was a substantial brick and timber waiting room with a canopy and a pitched slate roof. During the twentieth century, some changes were made to the goods yard layout. Arguably the greatest of these was the removal of the loop through the goods shed and its replacement with a simple siding behind the up platform so that access to the goods yard was now only from the east end. The building of a number of woollen mills on the north side of the line in the late nineteenth century gave rise to a private siding to Waverley Mills, accessed from the goods yard. The second stage of the line, from Innerleithen Station to Galashiels, opened on 18 June 1866. After that, most trains ran the whole length of the line.

A mile further on and some ten miles from Galashiels was Walkerburn Station. Unfortunately, at the time that the second extension of the Peebles Railway opened to Galashiels, Walkerburn was incomplete and its opening had to be delayed until 15 January 1867. Walkerburn had only a single platform on the up side, to the west of the level crossing. Originally, the platform had been on the other side of the line and what later became the stationmaster's house was the original station building. Following a tragic accident in about 1892 when a prominent Peebles builder was run over and killed by the train he was rushing to catch, the station was moved to the other side of the line. The new station building was of brick construction surmounted by a slate roof, in the same standard style as Cardrona but with a substantial veranda, beneath which passengers could shelter. This building contained waiting rooms and toilets as well as a booking office. There was also a timber-built footbridge adjacent to the level crossing, for passengers' use when the level crossing was closed. In addition, there was a stone-built stationmaster's house built with an 'L' plan, opposite the station building itself and again roofed with slate. The goods yard itself was quite commodious and consisted of two sidings spaciously laid out. The nearer of these two loops to the running line also served a substantial stone-built, slate-roofed goods shed as well as a loading bank, while the other accommodated a two-ton crane. The original signal box appears to have been replaced in 1895 by a new one on the up side of the line, a little to the west of the platform, controlling both the level crossing and the entrance to the goods yard.

The next station as the line wended its way south-east was Thornielee. Originally the station was titled Thornilee, but that mistake was corrected in March 1872 when it was re-titled Thornielee. The station had a single platform on the up side with a stone-built and slate-roofed station building containing both a stationmaster's house and ticket office at the east end of the platform. Thornielee never boasted a signal box, though it did possess a goods yard, the entrance to which was located just off the western end of the platform. This small goods yard was furnished with a loop and a loading bank. In about 1900 two railway cottages were built at the back of the goods yard. Never busy, it came as a surprise to nobody when the station was closed to both passengers and goods on 6 November 1950.

The next stop, albeit an unadvertised one, was at Angling Club Halt, opened in 1898 for the benefit of the members of the Edinburgh Angling Club who wanted to use The Nest, a cottage owned by that Club. Access to The Nest from Angling Club Halt was by way of a short path along the side of the track to the north-east corner of the cottage's grounds. The stop itself consisted of a simple timber-faced cinder platform with a timber-built waiting shelter but devoid of any other embellishments. There were no goods facilities. Ordinary passengers were allowed to use the halt provided they were in possession of a ticket to the next station past it and gave due notice to the guard.

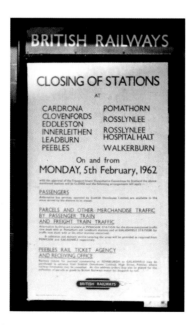

Closure notice for stations along the Peebles loop. (*G. N. Turbbull, WRHA Archive*)

The last station before Galashiels was at Clovenfords. Early maps (dating from before 1880) show no goods yard here and only a very small station building. According to Ordnance Survey maps, that situation had changed by the turn of the century some twenty years later, and a larger station building as well as a small goods yard had been provided. Additionally, a signal box is shown between the sidings and the running line at the north end of the platform, which was on the down side; the signal box appears to have been very short-lived. Sitting atop the brick-faced platform was an L-shaped station building with a slated, pitched roof which included an integral sheltered waiting area. At the Galashiels end of the station was a loop which in turn gave access to a loading bank and a single other siding containing a crane.

The Galashiels line to Peebles finally joined the Waverley Route at Kilnknowe Junction, about a mile north of Galashiels. There was never a station here, though before the 1930s re-signalling of Galashiels there was a signal box.

The Polton and Penicuik branches both closed to passengers on the same day, 10 September 1951, though both were retained for goods traffic until 18 May 1964 and 27 March 1967 respectively. On the complete closure of the Penicuik branch, the track was lifted all the way back to Hardengreen Junction. The remains of the Leadburn to Dolphinton branch went out of use in 1950, though it was another ten years before the track was lifted. The Peebles loop was dieselised in 1958, with a much improved service, including some extra trains providing an outer suburban service from Edinburgh as far as Rosewell & Hawthornden, though ultimately the new trains still failed to generate enough new income to save the line and the Peebles loop closed to goods and passenger traffic from Monday 5 February 1962, the last passenger train being the 11.00 p.m. (Saturdays only), arriving at Galashiels at 00.29 a.m. A steam-hauled special had passed over the line earlier in the day. The service to Roswell & Hawthornden lasted a little longer, ending on 10 September.

Journey's start from the perspective of this book – Edinburgh Waverley. The east end of Waverley Station is shown here as an unidentified J37 makes its way south towards Carton Tunnel with a mixed freight transfer. From the extreme left, just out of shot, we have the suburban platforms; the through platforms, Nos 10 and 11, on the south side just above the guards van; the Waverley platforms, Nos 9 and 8; three further sets of bay platforms, 7 and 6, 5 and 4 and 3 and 2 for the Leith and East Lothian services; and finally through platforms Nos 1 and 19 with the north side through loop and sidings. Although continuous in construction, both the north and south through platforms were (and still are) split into two sections and numbered accordingly. (*R. B. MacCartney Collection*)

With the construction of Millerhill Marshalling Yard all trace of the platforms at Millerhill have gone, with only the station building remaining. The truncated remains of the Glencorse Branch continued to see traffic to Bilston Glen Colliery until the early 1990s, when final closure of the remaining branch came. Today a single line and a run-round facility still exists for turning trains on the triangle and accessing the wagon repair shops, although it has seen increasingly little use in recent times. As can be seen, the site has become heavily overgrown. (*I. MacIntosh*)

Millerhill was the first station on leaving the East Coast Main Line for the Waverley Route. It opened along with the Hawick Branch of the NBR in September of 1847 and closed to passengers in 1955. Millerhill only served a sparse rural community until the opening of the Glencorse branch raised its status to a junction station, with passengers changing trains here. (*Bill Lynn Collection*)

From the mid-1980s the Down sorting yards were taken out of use and the South Down and Waverley Route lines were converted into the Electrification Depot for the works to electrify the East Coast Main Line. On completion of these works the area largely fell out of use, only the Glencorse Branch being left in use until 1994, and the remaining stub was used to turn trains on the triangle at Millerhill Yard and access the wagon repair works until relatively recently. (*I. MacIntosh*)

Millerhill South Downs was the point where up and down freights for the East Coast Main Line were run-round for arrival/departure from the new 1962 Millerhill Marshalling Yard. This photo shows a pair of Clayton Type 1s, with D8605 leading, working in multiple, on a Dundee to Blackpool Summer Saturdays only special just passing the old Millerhill Station and the junction for the Glencorse Branch and the South Downs on 25 June 1966. (*G. N. Turnball, WRHA Archive*)

Today, the New Borders Railway is beginning to take shape here at Sheriffhall, with the closure of the footpath to Hardengreen making way once again for DMU traffic, albeit to Galashiels and Tweedbank. (*I. MacIntosh*)

A two-car DMU is seen skirting the woods at Sheriffhall in 1966 on its way from Hawick to Edinburgh. Although the Peebles loop had closed by this date, these units were used on the Peebles Loop services from their introduction in Scotland in 1955. Although far more economic to operate and maintain than the steam traction they replaced, they still could not prevent the closure of the line due to dwindling passenger receipts. (*G. N. Turnball*)

Eskbank Station formed one of the largest conurbations on leaving Edinburgh for passenger receipts, the view south here unfortunately showing empty platforms outwith the peak period. The typical 1950s paraphernalia of posters and signs aimed at attracting custom can be seen, as can the general levels of cleanliness for the commuting traffic. Through the bridge lies Hardengreen Junction, the divergence of the Peebles Loop proper, as we will see. (*Bill Lynn Collection*)

An elevated shot is reproduced here as the trackbed is now under preparation for the New Borders Railway. The footbridge was gifted to the WRHA for reuse at their Whitrope headquarters in 2012, as mentioned in our previous book. It is, however, good to see the general clearance of the site much in evidence and a more accessible station site being prepared beyond bridge 15 at Hardengreen Junction. (*I. MacIntosh*)

The up line waiting platform at Eskbank Station is displayed here. In this post-closure study taken by Roy in 1969, we can see the general failing in the upkeep of the structures on site given their lack of maintenance, although they are essentially intact. (*Roy G. Perkins*)

As mentioned in the previous caption, the footpath has now been closed to the public and I offer this shot from my 2005 archive instead. Although unfortunately not a direct comparison, it does display the current general condition of the site and the demolition of everything bar the platforms. As mentioned, the footbridge has been removed to Whitrope and I promise not to mention it again, maybe? The site has since benefitted from vegetation management, as can be seen from the previous photographic comparison. (*I. MacIntosh*)

The new Eskbank Station is shortly to be constructed within the area of Hardengreen Junction. The modern screening of housing, although showing the reason for a new station here, completely hides all trace of this location's former importance. (*I. MacIntosh*)

A Hawick-bound DMU clears Hardengreen Junction on its way south, calling at all stations to Hawick. Hardengreen Junction Signal Box stands above the rear vehicle and the Up Yard is off to the right. The Clayton type 1 (later class 17 and never a successful type of traction) stands on the remains of the Pebbles Loop. (*I. MacIntosh Collection*)

The south end of the Hardengreen Junction complex gives a good overview of the size and role it performed. At the very top of the picture is the signal box, with the Peebles Loop leaving to the left, the down sidings with loaded coal traffic stabled and to the right the goods sidings for Eskbank and the general area. A WD 2-8-0 heads south along the up Waverley main line with a mixed train hardly befitting of its tractive effort. (*I. MacIntosh Collection*)

As can be seen, the new housing development has completely laid waste to the original Peebles Loop formation. Back-filling of the cutting and south end sidings almost renders the comparative unrecognisable, with only the trees on the horizon tying the scenes together. (*I. MacIntosh*)

Lasswade Station on the Poulton Branch. Lasswade and Broomieknowe stations, along with Bonnyrigg on the Peebles Loop, all served the area of Lasswade. Lasswade and Broomieknowe were situated on the NBR Poulton Branch and the reason for Bonnyrigg being so named was to avoid confusion on the timetable. A short tunnel separated the rather less well appointed stations from their near relative. (*Bill Lynn Collection*)

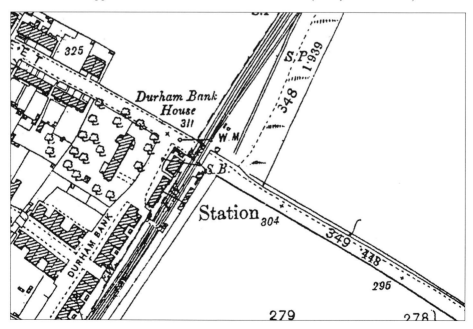

Bonnyrigg Station from the 1893 25-inch Ordnance Survey map. (*Iain MacIntosh Collection*)

Bonnyrigg was the first station on the Peebles Loop after leaving the main line. Built as an afterthought to provide passenger facilities for nearby Lasswade, it opened a month after the railway first saw passenger traffic. This is demonstrated by the simplicity of the structures when compared to other stations on the route. (*Bill Lynn Collection*)

Bonnyrigg survived the closure of the route to Peebles, remaining open for goods traffic until the Penicuik Line closed in 1965. The yard lay on the other side of the level crossing and although the platforms survive on the west side, the goods yard is now a housing development. (*Iain MacIntosh*)

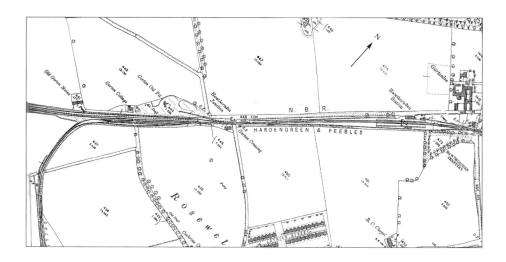

Rosewell & Hawthornden Station from the 1897 25-inch Ordnance Survey map. (*Iain MacIntosh Collection*)

An Edinburgh-bound service calls at Rosewell & Hawthornden's neat platforms. (*Bill Lynn Collection*)

Rosewell & Hawthornden with the last day special. Hawthornden Junction, a little to the west, marked the end of the double track section as the Penicuik Branch departed and the Whitehill colliery and sidings parted company with the through route. A loop existed behind the up platform, resulting in the double bridge seen above. (*Bill Lynn Collection*)

Rosewell & Hawthorden lingered on for passenger service for another seven months following the line's closure. From this point the remaining line to Penicuik survived but traffic was no longer catered for here and the line to Hardengreen was singled. The platforms remain devoid of all furniture and buildings and are heavily overgrown. (*Iain MacIntosh*)

The old platforms at Rosewell & Hawthornden lurk forgotten in the undergrowth and a tarmac path now runs along the formation, a very welcome improvement over my first visit in 2003. (*Iain MacIntosh*)

The neat and pleasant nature of this rural station can be seen, with the sparse goods yard beyond in 1953. The footbridge and the later addition dominate the scene, with the station building and small waiting shelter in evidence. (*Bill Lynn Collection*)

Rosslynlee was nominally built to serve Roslin and the famous Roslin Chapel. In actual fact, Roslin lay some two miles away and the station served several small villages around the area. A single platform and siding were provided to service the traffic needs of the area. Roslynlee closed along with the line in February of 1962. (*Bill Lynn Collection*)

Now a private dwelling, the station has been sensitively converted and the driveway and garden now occupy the former track bed. (*WRHA Archive*)

Rosslynlee Hospital Halt was provided in 1958 for DMU traffic to the hospital. Lasting barely four years, it has to be one of the shortest lived stations in Scotland. Measuring only 20 metres long, it required skill for the driver to stop with the door alongside the platform. (*Bill Lynn Collection*)

All that now remains is the gap in the wall for access to the hospital grounds from the former platform site. The track bed is now overgrown and wet in places. (*Iain MacIntosh*)

Pomathorn is now a private residence; trees grow along the former trackbed and the road level has been raised over the years. (*WRHA Archive*)

Pomathorn was built to serve Penicuik, half a mile to the north. A passing loop had been provided but by the date of this photograph it had been removed. Only one platform was ever provided despite the loop line. A goods yard consisting of three sidings was provided, which was somewhat substantial compared to the single sidings provided at other locations. All of this remained open until the line's closure, although it was designated as a halt by then. (*Bill Lynn Collection*)

Pomathorn for Penicuik, as the running-in board reads in this 1956 view. By this date Pomathorn was an unstaffed halt. The style and size of the station buildings provided is well demonstrated in this scene, reasonably busy for a remote halt. (*Bill Lynn Collection*)

The station buildings still stand in private use and the waiting room still exists beyond the main house. The track bed is now a green corridor of shrubs and trees. (*WRHA Archive*)

The only activity at Pomathorn is a short rake of mineral wagons in No. 1 siding. By this time Pomathorn was classified as an unstaffed halt. (*Bill Lynn Collection*)

A view in
towards
Peebles
through the
deserted
station of
Pomathorn.
(*Bill Lynn
Collection*)

Leadburn opened with the line in 1855 and had a lifespan of just under 100 years to passengers, closing in 1955. The remaining freight traffic succumbing with the line's closure. The following selection of photographs illustrates the expansion of the site when the Dolphinton Branch opened in 1864. The north end of the station complex is seen here in 1953, with the well tended platforms and lofty signal box. (*Bill Lynn Collection*)

The site lay derelict for many years before a picnic area was created and the site tidied up. The substantial remains of the platforms now provide a pleasant resting area for the passing tourist traffic. (*Iain MacIntosh*)

Today all the buildings at Leadburn have been swept away, leaving the cut back up platform and the down platform. The area has been landscaped and shrubs planted, although with spring taking so long to arrive this year, the area looks a little sorry for itself. (*Iain MacIntosh*)

The commanding signal box stands high above the surrounding station infrastructure. On the left is the up platform for Peebles with the down for Edinburgh in the foreground. The bay platform for Dolphinton traffic is through the bridge and to the right. A long lye siding was provided behind the up platform. (*Bill Lynn Collection*)

This end of the site has benefitted the most from landscaping. The slope in the middle is all that remains of the bay platform. (*Iain MacIntosh*)

An early view here of the south-west end of Leadburn Station, with the goods yard and Dolphinton bay shown. A turntable had originally been provided at the end of the bay but was taken out of use with the branch's closure in 1933. The bay then became another siding and was used to stable mineral wagons for Macbie Hill on the remaining stub of the branch. (*Bill Lynn Collection*)

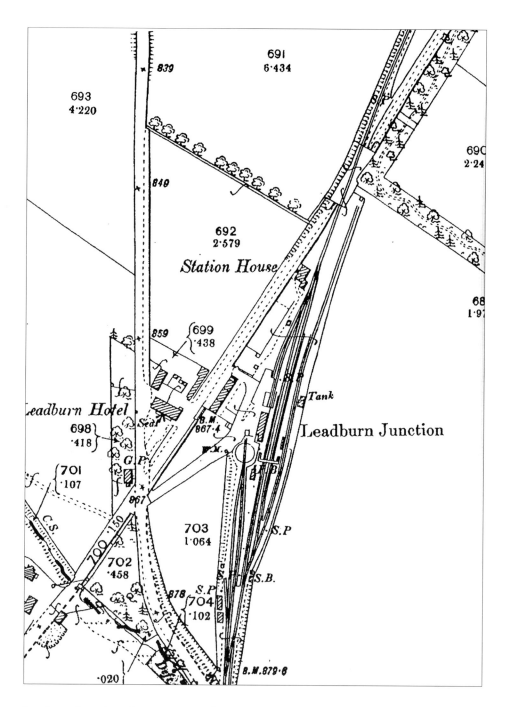

Leadburn Junction, shown in an Ordnance Survey map from the 1890s. (*Iain MacIntosh Collection*)

The view north through Leadburn shows the long lye leading off to the right. The box had started to suffer and started crumbling, prompting a replacement to be built; this is shown under construction below and in front of the original, which was still in commission. (*Bill Lynn Collection*)

The extent to which the up platform has been cut back becomes noticeable here as Dave and Abi inspect the site. The moss is starting to claim this end of the site now. (*Iain MacIntosh*)

A general view north through the station from a departing Galashiels service. The new signal box is taking shape and the yard and cut down Dolphinton bay are home to some stabled mineral wagons. (*Bill Lynn Collection*)

A general contemporary view north, with the full length of the picnic area and interpretation board shown. (*Iain MacIntosh*)

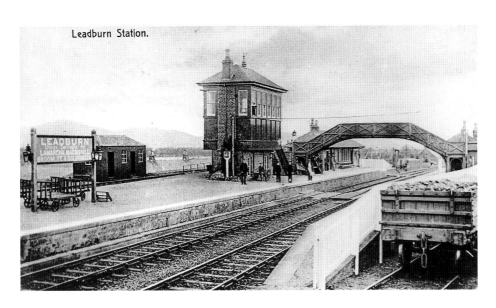

Leadburn Station.

Leadburn became the junction for the branch to Dolphinton in July of 1864, the station running-in board reading 'Leadburn change for Lamancha, Macbie Hill, Broomilee and Dolphinton'. This early twentieth-century view north-east shows old North British wooden open wagons, including wooden buffers in the up siding to the right, the then new signal box and through platforms in the centre and the small goods yard and Dolphinton Branch bay platform to the left. (*Bill Lynn Collection*)

The Dolphinton Branch became an early casualty of economics closing in 1933. Some goods traffic did see some of the branch retained through until 1950 with final lifting of the remaining track in 1961. Leadburn fared little better with passenger traffic being withdrawn in 1955 and freight upon clousure of the route on 5 February 1962. Today, a car park and picnic area occupy what remains of the site's railway archaeology. (*Iain MacIntosh*)

38

Eddleston was a planned village constructed in the eighteenth century and was a natural choice for a station. Indeed, it was the first station on leaving the Lothian suburbs to be located within the village it served. Originally constructed as single platform along with the line, the need for passing places soon became obvious and a second platform was provided. The view south in this early twentieth century image shows the well appointed station and staff. (*Bill Lynn Collection*)

Unfortunately, due to new development a true comparative cannot be achieved. The contemporary shot does show the main station building in immaculate condition and the platforms in-filled to form a garden. (*Iain MacIntosh*)

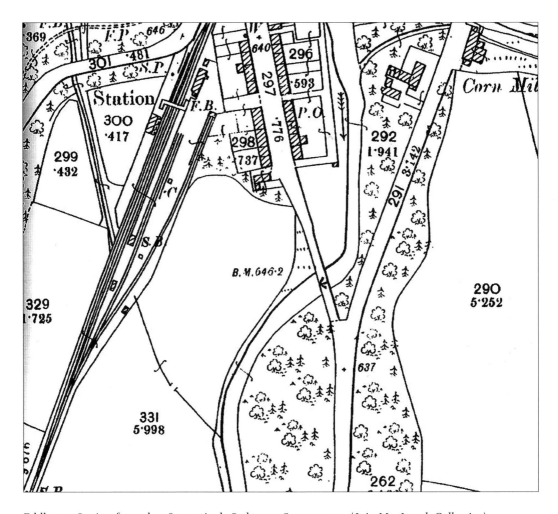

Eddleston Station from the 1897 25-inch Ordnance Survey map. (*Iain MacIntosh Collection*)

The whole goods yard has now been redeveloped but the sensitive extension to the original station building stands out from the more mundane architecture, a real credit to the station's owner. (*Iain MacIntosh*)

The view north after the passing loop was decommissioned. A refuge siding remained in place for shunting and the goods yard still continued to see traffic. Note the camping coach to the rear of the platform. (*Bill Lynn Collection*)

Again, the well-maintained buildings are shown to advantage, as is the general cleanliness and pride the owner bestows on the property, with the evidence of winter pruning ready for disposal. (*Iain MacIntosh*)

A general view south again after the simplification of the station and infrastructure. The platforms and gardens are still well tended. (*Bill Lynn Collection*)

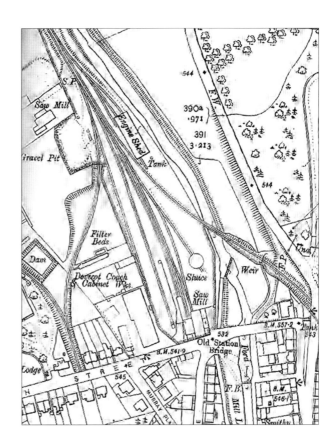

Peebles Old Station Goods Yard and engine shed from the 1908 25-inch Ordnance Survey map. (*Iain MacIntosh Collection*)

The approach to Peebles, with an Edinburgh-bound DMU a minute or so into its journey. This area was originally the throat to the original station of 1855. In 1864 the new through line opened and the old station site became the north-end goods yard referred to as the Old Station Goods Yard. A branch once served March Street Mill and the tracks can still be found within the sets of the roadway inside its grounds. (*Bill Lynn Collection*)

Today the ground levels have been altered and it is difficult to find the correct view point, although the footbridge in the background still crosses the river at the same location. A new housing development and sports fields stand to the right. (*Iain MacIntosh*)

The area is now a compound and works unit and I must confess that, although I found the correct location, I pointed the camera in the wrong direction. I should have been facing 45 degrees to the right. (*Iain MacIntosh*)

The signal box controlling the junction to the Old Station Goods Yard stood by Eddleston Water, a short distance to the north of the original station site. This controlled the access to the yard, the shed and the direct Galashiels route via the new 1864 station. (*Bill Lynn Collection*)

Peebles Engine Shed stood alongside the new line to the north of Old Station Goods Yard. The new line passed alongside in the foreground before crossing over Eddleston Water and squeezing its way into Peebles. (*Bill Lynn Collection*)

The area of Old Station Goods Yard has now been completely redeveloped with flats and a large supermarket. No signs remain to indicate the transport history of this location. (*Iain MacIntosh*)

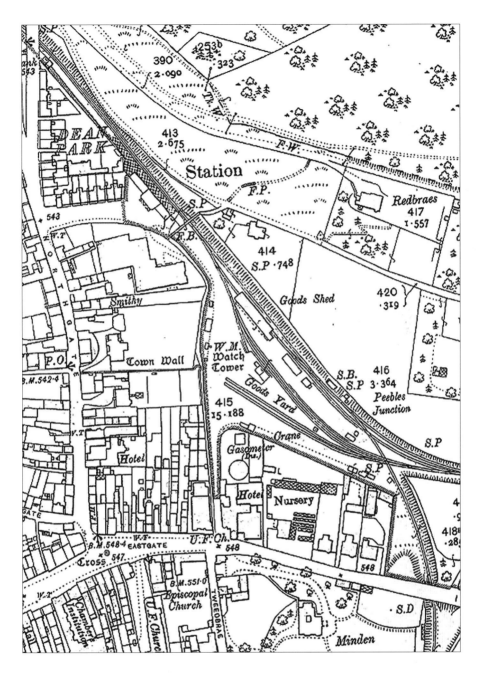

Peebles East Station from the 1908 25-inch Ordnance Survey map. (*Iain MacIntosh Collection*)

The main station building of the Galashiels extension, just off Northgate, Peebles, was a sympathetic but imposing building. Built for the extension in 1864, the building survived closure until the 1970s saw it demolished and swept away to make room for road improvements. This early twentieth century view shows attendant horse drawn carriages awaiting their trade. (*Bill Lynn Collection*)

Today, all trace of the station building and infrastructure have been swept away to make room for the A703. A formal garden adorns the former cutting side. (*Iain MacIntosh*)

A closer view of the main station building at Peebles, showing well the detail and its imposing nature. Some of the staff have posed in their uniforms for the photographer. (*Bill Lynn Collection*)

Today, although neat and tidy with the gardens and flower beds, nothing exists of the station. A short distance to the left, however, there is a plaque and representation of a steam engine to commemorate the railway's passing. (*Iain MacIntosh*)

The A703 Edinburgh Road follows the route of the railway past Dean Road end, about the only link between the historic and contemporary views. No footbridge is in place today – there is just a pair of bollards marking a pedestrian crossing and a hike up the bank on the right to meet Venlaw Quarry Road. (*Iain MacIntosh*)

A view of the south end of the station buildings and platform side taken from the window of a departing Galashiels-bound train. The footbridge linked Dean Park and Redbraes. (*Bill Lynn Collection*)

A fine historic study of an NBR steam engine bringing a service in for Galashiels. This early twentieth century photograph demonstrates well the patronage that the line enjoyed in the days before mass car ownership. It also highlights a lot of the detail features of the canopy and trackside façade. (*Bill Lynn Collection*)

Again, Edinburgh Road sweeps along through the site, but a mural of an old NBR engine adorns the wall beyond Dean Park Road. (*Iain MacIntosh*)

The new order arrives in the form of a diesel multiple unit for Galashiels. When first introduced to the line, some of these services extended to Kelso. Despite the new comfort and faster journey times, these units could not turn the tide and compete with growing road use, although it is pleasing to see this one with passengers alighting/joining the service. (*Bill Lynn Collection, Iain MacIntosh*)

Another view through the station, this time looking south. The platform length can be appreciated from this photograph and all the advertising hoardings in use. (*Bill Lynn Collection*)

Even without the attendant railway staff to keep the gardens in order, the local council workers have done a great job making the main route into and through Peebles a very pleasing and welcoming experience, to their great credit. (*Iain MacIntosh*)

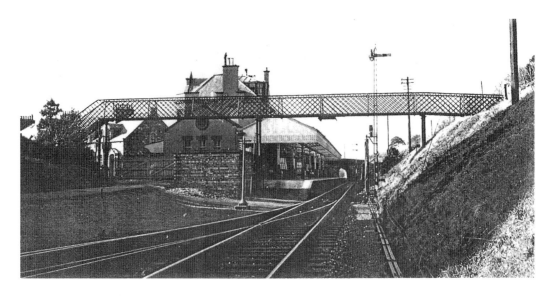

This comparative general view north through the station area shows the former Edinburgh Road bridge over the line at the point where it turns to cross Eddleston Water and join the original Peebles Railway. (*Bill Lynn Collection, Iain MacIntosh*)

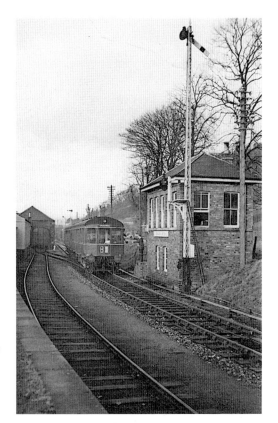

Peebles South box controlled the link line between the Caledonian station and the entrance into the goods yard at the south end of the station. A Galashiels-bound DMU has just passed the goods shed and is about to turn the corner after the signal box and run through the grounds of the Peebles Hydro. (*Bill Lynn Collection*)

The view towards the junction, showing the through-route curving around to the left for Galashiels and the link line to the Caledonian bisecting the goods yard lines. The squeezed in nature of the trackwork is evident as the line was constructed through quite a tight margin of the town as it turned from the valley of the Eddleston Water into the Tweed Valley. (*Bill Lynn Collection*)

Barely recognisable as the same location, without the clutter of the railway goods sidings and associated buildings, the area now feels very open. The route to Gala followed the low lying land to the left beyond the wall and the road follows the formation of the link line. (*Iain MacIntosh*)

Now one of the town's car parks occupies the site but the surviving weighbridge hut remains in the centre left of view, tying the scenes together. (*Iain MacIntosh*)

The full extent of the goods yard south end is displayed, with the intricate trackwork of the link line running through left to right. The goods yards were protected from the link by a signal just out of shot to the left and a catch point, which can just be made out at the bottom left with its catch rail above the running rail. (*Bill Lynn Collection*)

A general view north, demonstrating the crammed running line skirting the site and turning off to the right of scene. Peebles benefited from three goods yards in all and certainly couldn't be described as underserved in this respect. Again, today the scene is much altered, but the tall building in the centre ties the contemporary and historic studies. (*Bill Lynn Collection, Iain MacIntosh*)

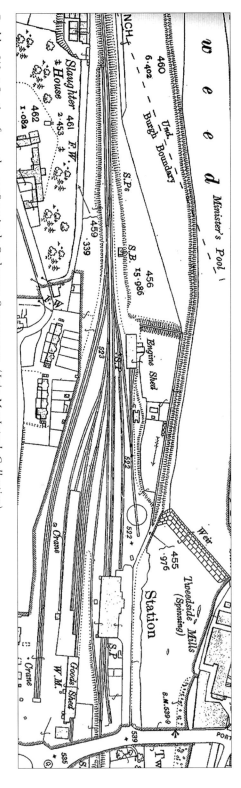

Peebles West Station from the 1908 25-inch Ordnance Survey map (*Iain MacIntosh Collection*)

The former site of Peebles West is today occupied by houses very pleasantly situated alongside the River Tweed. The former link chord now forms a walk alongside the Tweed, passing through the arch that still remains in the road bridge which crosses the river to Port Brae. (*Iain MacIntosh*)

The last passenger train is shown at Peebles West Station on 3 June 1950. The station continued to receive goods traffic from the former Caledonian main line via Broughton for a further four years, after which time the site only became accessible by rail from Peebles East via the link chord. This working continued until the final closure of the Peebles Loop in February of 1962. (*Bill Lynn Collection*)

More of the redevelopment is shown with the very pleasant and well maintained gardens on display. (*Iain MacIntosh*)

Another view of the last passenger train on departure. For what could have been a busy occasion, only two coaches are attached in the consist. (*Bill Lynn Collection*)

Today the view is unrecognisable but the long retaining wall built here by the Caledonian still exists. A footpath wends its way along the river side providing some beautiful vistas of the town. (*Iain MacIntosh*)

The last passenger train departs for Symington on the West Coast Main Line in June 1950. Although not the best quality of photographs, we thought them worthy of inclusion. The shed stands alongside the Tweed to the right with the bay platform, and the turntable is just out of view to the extreme right. (*Bill Lynn Collection*)

The trackbed at Cardrona now forms part of a golf course and is used to cross between courses. A large amount of development in line with these courses has taken place, with new housing and a large hotel having been built in recent times. (*Iain MacIntosh*)

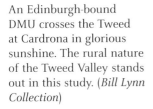

An Edinburgh-bound DMU crosses the Tweed at Cardrona in glorious sunshine. The rural nature of the Tweed Valley stands out in this study. (*Bill Lynn Collection*)

Cardrona station still stands, shrouded by trees, and the mortal remains of a permanent-way cabin decay at the side of the new long-distance footpath which is in the course of construction. (*Iain MacIntosh*)

Viewed from the rear of an Edinburgh-bound service, the sparse facilities and rural landscape stand out. The siding leading behind the station and the single wagon head shunt can be seen. (*Bill Lynn Collection*)

The contemporary view is actually from 2002 but demonstrates the current state of the surviving buildings. Now home to an ice cream shop, it still stands alongside a car park and the now much-widened road, which has resulted in the area being landscaped. (*WRHA Archive*)

The main station building and small signal box with the bridge over the Tweed in the distance make for a pleasing rural scene. Although small, the station is in immaculate condition. (*Bill Lynn Collection*)

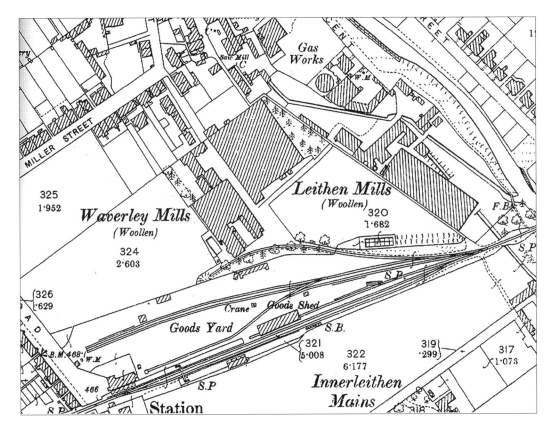

Innerleithen Station from the 1897 25-inch Ordnance Survey map. (*Iain MacIntosh Collection*)

An NBR service for Galashiels arrives at Innerleithen in the late 1880s. Innerleithen was a sizeable town and was home to several mills. As such, a fair-sized yard was provided and a private siding extended into Waverley Mill. (*Bill Lynn Collection*)

Today, the station building, all still extant, is surrounded by new builds and development. As such no direct comparison is possible but the station building can be clearly seen. (*Iain MacIntosh*)

The main station building stands substantially unaltered with the garden spreading over the trackbed. Beyond the fence the truncated remains of the up platform exist, and the yard has become home to industrial units. (*Iain MacIntosh*)

A view through the station towards Galashiels from the level crossing. The main station building stands to the left, with the additional platform staggered beyond to the right. Again, the pride of staff in the up keep of the station and gardens can be noted. (*Bill Lynn Collection*)

The lofty and somewhat spindly looking signal box stands at the end of the down platform as the track falls down gradient as it winds down the valley towards Walkerburn. (*Bill Lynn Collection*)

The industrial units occupy the formation beyond the station now. The down platform is still extant, providing a foundation for the building on the extreme right. The box stood just beyond. (*Iain MacIntosh*)

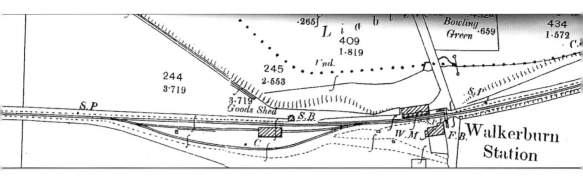

Walkerburn Station from the 1897 25-inch Ordnance Survey map. (*Iain MacIntosh Collection*)

A wonderful panoramic view of Walkerburn showing the railway following the sweep of the Tweed Valley and the station's proximity to the mill town it served. (*Bill Lynn Collection*)

The station buildings and platform survive and the yard area is now home to local business Glendinning Groundworks and I am indebted to them for allowing access to gain the contemporary photographs. (*Iain MacIntosh*)

Walkerburn Station was located on the opposite bank of the Tweed, just outside of Walkerburn, another mill town in the upper Tweed Valley centred on the wool trade. The station was actually six months late, opening on completion of the through route. (*Bill Lynn Collection*)

Walkerburn consisted of a single-storey station building and stationmaster's house. A single platform and two-road goods yard provided the necessary facilities for all traffic. The signal box was beyond the station on the road side and controlled the level crossing and access to the yard. (*Iain MacIntosh*)

The station building survives, although much altered, behind the screen of trees in the background and the platform within the yard area and formation are in use for storage of plant and materials for Glendinning Groundworks. (*Iain MacIntosh*)

Although tree growth impedes the view, all the structures survive in their new roles and the footprint of the site is obvious. Walkerburn itself has grown and is served now by the number 62 bus, plying the route of the erstwhile Peebles Loop. (*Iain MacIntosh*)

A general overview of the yard, with Walkerburn town clinging to the hill behind. The box was later moved to the east end of the site, by the level crossing. The substantial goods shed and busy sidings are a sign of the traffic generated from this small town. (*Bill Lynn Collection*)

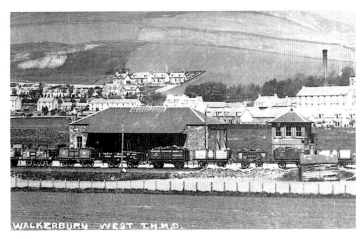

Walkerburn Goods Yard. (*Bill Lynn Collection*)

Walkerburn Station in flood. (*Bruce McCartney Collection*)

Thornielee Station was an early casualty, closing in 1950. No sizeable community existed, as evidenced by the single platform and the single siding provided for goods traffic. The station lies at the foot of the climb to Clovenfords, as evidenced by the gradient post on the right. (*Bill Lynn Collection*)

The station building survived and now forms a domestic residence and has had a sympathetic extension added to the platform side. (*WRHA Archive*)

Clovenfords was the last station before entering Galashiels. The station building survives here in a much altered state, surrounded by new housing development. A true comparative is not possible due to these new houses and the presence of a garage behind the photographer. (*Iain MacIntosh*)

Really just a village and only three miles or so from Galashiels, simple provision was made at Clovenfords for both goods and passenger traffic. The station was cut into the fell-side and opened up to a small but level yard and approach. (*Bill Lynn Collection*)

The encroachment of new housing at Clovenfords has altered the scene dramatically. It is somewhat hard to believe that this is a former railway at all, with the only nod towards it provided by the development's name, Station Yard. (*Iain MacIntosh*)

This general elevated shot towards Galashiels reveals the small yard and rural nature of the area. A steady climb had to be made from Galashiels to just west of Clovenfords in order to leave the Gala Water Valley and enter the Tweed Valley. (*Bill Lynn Collection*)

A view towards Galashiels from the platform showing the small yard beyond and the flank of Meigle Hill. The line was forced to climb the valley alongside the road between this and Mains Hill to access Clovenfords from Galashiels. (*Bill Lynn Collection*)

The photograph looks back through Clovenfords' empty platforms as a Galashiels-bound service departs. (*Bill Lynn Collection*)

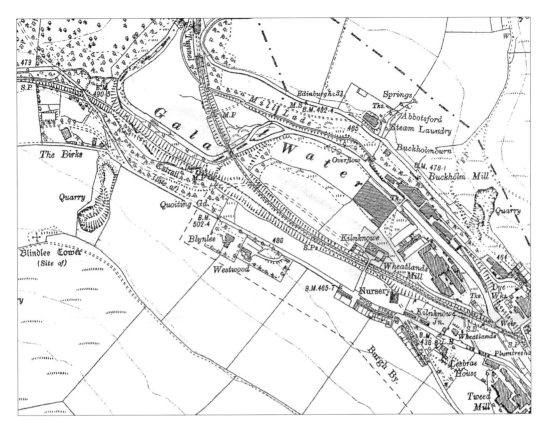

Kilknowe Junction Station from a 6-inch Ordnance Survey map from the 1890s. (*Iain MacIntosh Collection*)

Kilknowe became a junction with the opening of the full through Peebles line in 1866. Located a mile north of the town's station, it was the first open location available really to make a physical connection with the Waverley Route, it being heavily constrained and shoe horned to fit in here on in. This post-closure shot shows the Peebles Loop trackbed to the left of the closed but yet to be lifted Waverley line. (*Iain MacIntosh Collection*)

Contractors are seen at work in preparation for the New Borders Railway at Kilknowe Junction. The former Peebles line, now in use as a footpath, has been sectioned off from the physical works. (*Iain MacIntosh*)

The underbridge no 94 stretched beneath both the main lines of the Waverley Route and the branch for Peebles. The original Kilnknowe Junction box stood to the right and the Peebles Loop crossed nearest the camera. As can be seen from the contemporary view, road widening and re-alignment has taken place here and the original low bridge is going to have to be replaced by something with considerably more clearance. (*Roy G. Perkins, Iain MacIntosh*)

The view from Plumbtreehall north to Kilnknowe Junction shows a short freight entering the town. This pre-1933 shot shows Kilnknowe Junction signal box above the bridge over Gala Water. Wheatlands Mill stands in the background. (*Iain MacIntosh Collection*)

The same view in 2013, with vegetation clearance complete and the soon to be removed 'Black path' along the former route. Trains should return to service here again in 2015. (*Iain MacIntosh*)

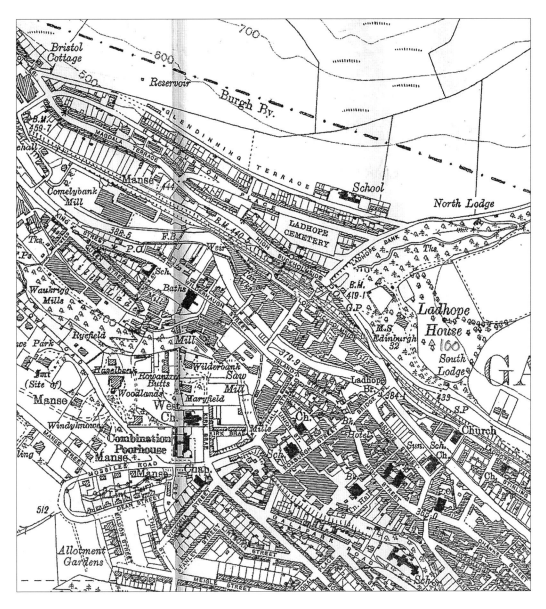

The north approaches to Galashiels Station taken from a 6-inch Ordnance Survey map from the 1890s. (*Iain MacIntosh Collection*)

The final crossing of Gala Water for the Waverley Route and the only encounter with it for Peebles services is seen here. Plumbtreehall road bridge stands in the background. From here in the route was heavily constrained on both sides, being squeezed in below Buckholmside and various mills, roads and the Gala Water itself. (*Roy G. Perkins*)

Bridge 95 over the Gala has been reduced in height but its central girders remain to carry the black path, whereas Plumbtreehall Bridge stands substantially unaltered. (*Iain MacIntosh*)

Plumbtreehall Bridge in close up. The line squeezes through below Magdala Terrace and High Buckholmeside, on the left, and Comelybank Mill behind the bridge to the right. A single line railway will once again negotiate its way through here in 2015. (*Roy G. Perkins, Iain MacIntosh*)

The route passes under this delightful footbridge as it threads through between High and Low Buckholmside. It is hoped this structure is to survive the return of rail traffic once more. (*Roy G. Perkins, Iain MacIntosh*)

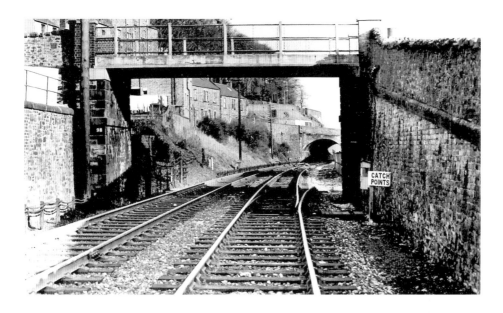

One of the only overbridges to have succumbed to demolition since the line's closure used to link High and Low Buckholmside and carried a lane between the two. Immediately beyond was Bridge 99 over Ladhope Burn, which is now a culvert, and beyond is the north portal of Ladhope Tunnel. The catch points had originally led into Patersons' number two siding. Today, the area is landscaped and the mills have made way for urban development. (*Roy G. Perkins, Iain MacIntosh*)

The Ladhope Tunnel brought the line under the A7 Edinburgh Road and marked the final approach to Galashiels Station. The high retaining walls replaced the original walls, which collapsed in December 1916, bringing some 70 yards of the original wall down, blocking the line. Fortunately, no injuries were sustained and the replacement wall stands fast to this day. With the closure of the route, the A7 was widened slightly to ease the bottlenecks out and as a result part of the portal face was obscured. Works in preparation for the new line have resulted in the construction of this new retaining wall to the left of the contemporary view. (*Roy G. Perkins, Iain MacIntosh*)

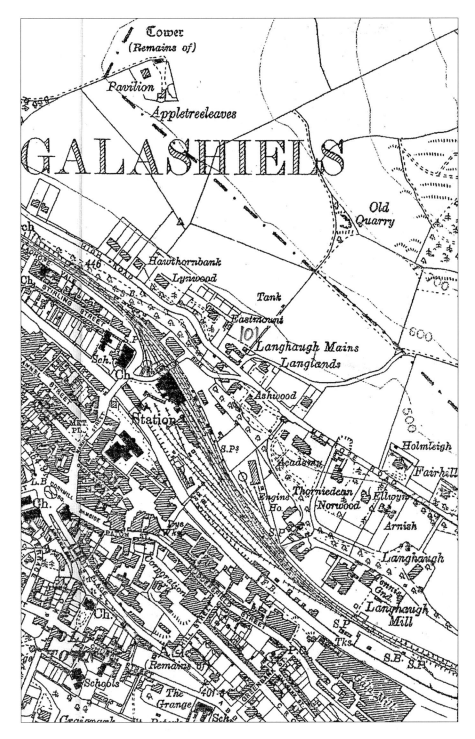

Galashiels Station and goods yard from a 6-inch Ordnance Survey map from the 1890s. (*Iain MacIntosh Collection*)

The north end of the station complex, demonstrating the tightly packed-in nature of the approach, squeezed between the main road and the town and running along the valley floor, flanked by Galalaw Fell. The line approached Galashiels Station from Ladhope below a large engineers' brick retaining wall before going through a tight reverse curve to enter the station. (*Roy G. Perkins*)

The new station is to be built alongside the road, on the straight in the background, providing an interchange with the bus station. In this contemporary photograph taken from the new Station Brae Bridge, the somewhat easier curve of the new line can be discerned. (*Iain MacIntosh*)

During the re-signalling and redevelopment of Galashiels Station in the 1930s, the north end bay gave way to what became a signature feature of the station – its north end gardens. Here a Sulzer type 2 awaits the road with a stopping train for Edinburgh alongside the gardens. (*WRHA Archive*)

With the subsequent redevelopment of the area, these gardens have made way for new gardens, this time flanking the new road system at Station Brae. The new line is to be threaded along below the trees. (*Iain MacIntosh*)

This location is now the car park of a health centre as the new formation of Station Brae climbs to cross over the replacement bridge. (*Iain MacIntosh*)

Journey's end for a Galashiels via Peebles service from Edinburgh as it rests in platform 3. The former Station Brae Bridge straddles all lines in the background. (*N. G. Turnbull, WRHA Archive*)

The shed site now lies empty alongside a supermarket, which occupies the majority of the site. Provision of space for the new line was part of the planning consent and the route from the new Galashiels Station to Tweedbank will see rail traffic passing here once more. (*Iain MacIntosh*)

Glen Lyon seen resting on shed at Galashiels. Galashiels provided locomotives for goods and passenger traffic on the Selkirk Branch, Peebles Loop and of course the Waverley Route. The shed was swept away shortly after closure and the site was re-developed. (*WRHA Archive*)

WAVERLEY ROUTE HERITAGE ASSOCIATION
MEMBERSHIP APPLICATION & DONATION FORM

Full Name
Address (Line 1)
Address (Line 2)
Address (Line 3)
Postcode

Age (if under 18)   Signature of Parent/Guardian required below

Telephone No
Email address

Any relevant skills ?

Please state whether membership application, donation or both (tick):
☐ Adult Membership (18 to 60 years) £20.00
☐ Senior (60 & over) & Junior Membership (Under 18s) £16.00
☐ Family Membership (2+2) £35.00

☐ Optional Donation £

Cheque/Postal Order Total £

Name of Parent/Guardian for under 18s......................................
Signature of Parent/Guardian ....

Please make cheques payable to 'WAVERLEY ROUTE HERITAGE ASSOCIATION'

I may be interested in the following (tick):
☐ Voluntary work - permanent way, maintenance, planning, research etc
☐ Representing WRHA at various events

Signature of applicant .... Date....................................

Please send this completed form, enclosing payment, to:

WRHA MEMBERSHIP SECRETARY, 41 GLENEAGLES DRIVE, CARLISLE, CUMBRIA. CA3 9PX

Personal details will be held for WRHA internal use only, in compliance with the Data Protection Act 1998.

Acknowledgements

The authors wish to express their thanks and gratitude to the following people for their assistance and encouragement.

Bruce McCartney, Bill Lynn and the WRHA for their invaluable photographic provision and assistance. Jane and Paul Langley, Marcus and Bo Day and big Dave Smith along with Abi the 'lookout dog' for transport assistance.

Andrew and Sarah MacIntosh, Janet and Lawson Short, Trisha Perkins, Nicola Graham and Louis Archard for encouragement, assistance and above all tolerance.

All the owners of the private sites visited for their generosity and interest.

And finally a special thank you to Grahame Hood for providing invaluable local knowledge and generally pointing us in the right direction.

All photographs have the originators name beside them.

A warm thank you to all.

Roy G. Perkins and Iain MacIntosh.

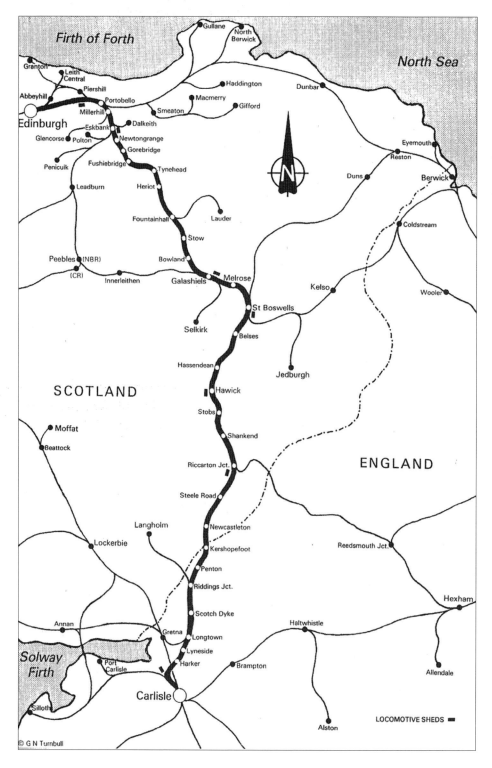

The railways of the Borders, showing the Waverley Route between Edinburgh and Carlisle and the Peebles loop branching off from it. (*G. N. Turnbull and the WRHA Archive*)